W9-CSB-560

Sunshine

by Ann Herriges

BELLWETHER MEDIA · MINNEAPOLIS, MN

Note to Librarians, Teachers, and Parents:

Blastoff! Readers are carefully developed by literacy experts and combine standards-based content with developmentally appropriate text.

Level 1 provides the most support through repetition of high-frequency words, light text, predictable sentence patterns, and strong visual support.

Level 2 offers early readers a bit more challenge through varied simple sentences, increased text load, and less repetition of high-frequency words.

Level 3 advances early-fluent readers toward fluency through increased text and concept load, less reliance on visuals, longer sentences, and more literary language.

Whichever book is right for your reader, Blastoff! Readers are the perfect books to build confidence and encourage a love of reading that will last a lifetime!

This edition first published in 2007 by Bellwether Media.

No part of this publication may be reproduced in whole or in part without written permission of the publisher. For information regarding permission, write to Bellwether Media Inc., Attention: Permissions Department, Post Office Box 1C, Minnetonka, MN 55345-9998.

Library of Congress Cataloging-in-Publication Data
Herriges, Ann.
  Sunshine / By Ann Herriges.
    p. cm. — (Weather) (Blastoff! readers)
Summary: "Simple text and supportive images introduce beginning readers to the characteristics of sunshine. Intended for students in kindergarten through third grade." Includes bibliographical references and index.
  ISBN-10: 1-60014-028-9 (hardcover : alk. paper)
  ISBN-13: 978-1-60014-028-0 (hardcover : alk. paper)
  1. Sunshine—Juvenile literature. 2. Weather—Juvenile literature. I. Title. II. Series. III. Series: Herriges, Ann. Weather.

QC911.2.H47 2007
  551.5'271—dc22   2006010305

Text copyright © 2007 by Bellwether Media.
Printed in the United States of America.

Table of Contents

Sunshine brings light and heat to the world.

Sunshine makes the
weather too.

Sunshine covers half of the
earth at a time. The earth spins.
Different parts of the earth move
into and out of the sun's light.

On one side of the earth it is day.
Heat from the sun warms the air.

On the other side of the earth it is night. The air becomes cooler after the sun goes down.

Rays of sunshine heat the **atmosphere**. The atmosphere is the air around the earth.

The rays heat some parts of the atmosphere more than others. The warmer air is lighter. It rises.

Cooler air is heavy. It flows into spaces where the warm air was. This moving air is the wind.

Sunshine heats water on the earth.
Tiny drops of water rise into the
air. They gather together
to make **clouds**.

Rain or snow falls from clouds.
Sometimes the sun and rain
make a rainbow.

Places near the **equator** get the most sunshine. This area is around the middle of the earth.

The sun rises high in the sky at the equator. Sunshine makes the air hot.

The top and bottom of the earth get the least sunshine. The sun stays low in the sky.

There is not much sunshine to heat the air. It is always cold.

Sunshine is different during each **season**. In June, more sunshine falls on the top half of the earth. It is summer there.

At the same time, the bottom half of the earth gets less sunshine. It is winter there.

In December, less sunshine falls
on the top half of the earth.
It is winter there.

The bottom half of the earth gets more sunshine now. It is summer there. The top half and bottom half of the world have **opposite** seasons.

Glossary

atmosphere—a mixture of gases around the earth that cannot be seen

cloud—tiny drops of water or crystals of ice that float together in the air

equator—an imaginary line around the middle of the earth; the equator is halfway between the top and the bottom of the earth.

opposite—to be located at the different ends or directly across from one another

ray—a narrow beam of light

season—one of the four parts of the year; the seasons are spring, summer, fall, and winter.

To Learn More

AT THE LIBRARY

Ganeri, Anita. *Sunshine*. Milwaukee, Wis.: Gareth Stevens, 2005.

Gibbons, Gail. *Weather Words and What They Mean*. New York: Holiday House, 1990.

Miles, Elizabeth. *Sunshine*. Chicago: Heinemann Library, 2005.

Sherman, Josepha. *Sunshine: A Book about Sunlight*. Minneapolis, Minn.: Picture Window Books, 2003.

Williams, Judith. *How Does the Sun Make Weather?* Berkeley Heights, N.J.: Enslow, 2005.

ON THE WEB
Learning more about the weather is as easy as 1, 2, 3.

1. Go to www.factsurfer.com

2. Enter "weather" into search box.

3. Click the "Surf" button and you will see a list of related web sites.

With factsurfer.com, finding more information is just a click away.

Index

The photographs in this book are reproduced through the courtesy of: International Stock/Getty Images, front cover; Tony Craddock/Getty Images, p. 4; Telnove Olya, p. 5; Christi Matei, p. 6; Eric O'Connell/Getty Images, p. 7; phdpsx//Getty Images, pp. 8-9; Bryan Brazil, p. 10; Vladimir Pomortzeff, p. 11; Jessica Bethke, p. 12; Olga Drozdova, p. 13; V Tupinamba, pp. 14-15; Frans Lemmens/Getty Images, pp. 16-17; Emmerich-Webb/Getty Images, p. 18; Medford Taylor/Getty Images, p. 19; Joy Strotz, p. 20; George Kamper/Getty Images, p. 21.